ETHICAL DEBATES

The Debate About
Immigration

CATH SENKER

rosen publishing's
rosen central

New York

Published in 2008 by The Rosen Publishing Group, Inc.
29 East 21st Street, New York, NY 10010

First Edition

Acknowledgments:

pp 4-5 Kim Jones: *Socialist Worker*, 20 May 2006; pp 12-13 Yueksal Tuncay: BBC News, Oct 30, 2001 by
Rob Broomby; pp 14-15 Arab News, Al-Jazeera, July 2003; www.aljazeerah.info; pp 22-23 Kobena: Making
the City Work: Low Paid Employment in London, 2005; pp 26-27 Pozzorubio: *Wall Street Journal*, May 22,
2001, © Dow Jones and Company Ltd; pp 33 (New York seamstresses) Multinational Monitor, October
2001; pp 36-7 racist attack: *Cambridge Evening News*, December 16, 2005, from   HYPERLINK
"http://www.islamophobia-watch.com" www.islamophobia-watch.com ; pp 40 Peter Hitchens: "The End
of Britain?" in *Double Crossings: Migration Now* (Index on Censorship, 2003); pp 44 Priya Ruth Gully
Cole (Author interview); pp 44 Faïza Guène: Authortrek.com and *Socialist Review*, May 2006.

Picture Acknowledgments: Cover photograph: Spectators (Chuck Savage/Corbis) Rob Huibers/ Panos
Pictures: 1, 42, Sipa Press/Rex Features: 4-5, 34, 35, 36, Khaled el Fiqi/EPA/Corbis: 6, Keren Su/Corbis: 8,
Mary Evans Picture Library: 9, Bettmann/ Corbis: 10, Corbis: 11, Reuters/Corbis: 13, 15, David H.
Wells/Corbis: 16, Ed Kashi/ Corbis: 19, 24, Peter Yates/Corbis: 20, Trygve Bolstad/Panos Pictures: 21, 22,
Caroline Penn/Corbis: 23, Andrew Drysdale/Rex Features: 25, T & L/Image Point/Corbis: 26, Howard
Davies/ Exile Images: 27, Andy Johnstone/ Panos Pictures: 28, Greg Smith/Corbis: 30, Steve Raymer/
Corbis: 31, Jim Sugar/Corbis: 32, Lorena Ros/Panos Pictures: 33, Justin Jin/Panos Pictures: 37, Bob
Krist/Corbis: 38, John Nordell/Image Works/Topfoto: 39, Nicholas Bailey/Rex Features: 40, Herbert
Pfarrhofer/ Corbis: 41, Paul Cooper/Rex Features: 43, Ronnie Kaufman/Corbis: 44, Tony Kyriacou/Rex
Features: 45.

Library of Congress Cataloging-in-Publication Data

Senker, Cath.
  The debate about Immigration / Cath Senker. -- 1st ed.
     p. cm. -- (Ethical debates)
  ISBN-13: 978-1-4042-3755-1 (lib. bdg.)
  ISBN-10: 1-4042-3755-0 (lib. bdg.)
  1. Emigration and immigration--Juvenile literature. I. Title.
  JV6035.S457 2007
  304.8--dc22
                              2006100312

Manufactured in China

contents

Immigration and the law

This case study shows some of the issues that surround the debate on immigration.

case study

Immigration and the law

On May 1, 2006, tens of thousands of people left school and work to attend mass protests around the U.S. They were demonstrating against a new immigration law, known as HR 4437, that would make it harder for people to move to the U.S. and would increase security at the borders. One young woman at the protest of around half a million people in Los Angeles was Kim Jones: "The day was amazing. I came all the way from Santa Ana [40 miles /60 km away] with my two friends on the metro. As soon as we got there all we saw were people wearing white in the streets. I could see everyone coming together as one, all fighting for one cause—blacks, Hispanics, whites, all sizes, and all ages..."

"I'm not an immigrant—I was born in Los Angeles. But my parents struggled and put their lives on the line to come across the border. Those fences didn't stop them and now they're legal, but still I feel that what many people in the U.S. are thinking is totally unfair. Many U.S. citizens say that immigrants need to get in line, that all they're doing is taking our money and our jobs. But immigrants have every right to be here, every right to want to live the 'American dream.'"

"We're all immigrants. If anything, the ones who deserve to be here are the Indians [the Native Americans]. But many people are ignorant and think that this place belongs to the whites, which is a total misunderstanding on their part."

"I just felt as if I had to be there with my people. We are all humans, and no one is alien. No matter what, we should all be entitled to the same rights. Immigrants work and pay taxes on food and clothes. They are human just like all U.S. citizens. If anything they should change the whole process of becoming legal because it takes 11 years and who really wants to wait that long?"

v i e w p o i n t s

"Many concerns that surround migration, such as loss of jobs, lower wages, increased welfare costs, and the belief that migration is spiraling out of control, are not only exaggerated or unfounded but contrary to evidence."
World Migration Report 2005

"Large-scale immigration has brought enormous social upheaval to France, Germany, Britain, and other European countries…an unblinkered society would seek to avoid such a fate. The only way to do so is to pursue a rigorous policy of immigration control."
Immigration Control Platform, Ireland

It's a fact

Experts estimate that around 250,00–300,000 undocumented migrants (illegal immigrants, see pages 6–7) enter the U.S each year, mostly from Mexico and Latin America.

▼ Crowds fill the street at the demonstration of May 1, 2006 in New York City. Around the U.S., immigrants and their supporters gathered for marches, prayers, and demonstrations.

What is immigration?

Migration—the movement of people from one country to another—occurs all the time and has done so throughout human history. Anyone who moves is a migrant. Immigration is a term used to describe the movement of people from their own country to settle permanently in another. They are immigrants to their new country, but have emigrated from their native country. In their home country, they are called emigrants. Legal immigrants are people who have permission to settle in their new country. Illegal immigrants (also called undocumented migrants) live in the new country illegally, according to immigration law. People who flee their country to escape war or persecution are known as refugees. If they have made a claim to stay in the country as refugees, they are also known as asylum seekers.

Push and pull factors

There are many reasons why people migrate. Some migration experts talk about "push and pull" factors. Push factors are bad things that make people leave their country. Perhaps they have little chance of making a good living. Their country may be affected by natural disasters, such as famine or floods, or by problems such as conflict, civil war, or political persecution. The decision to migrate is difficult and painful. It means leaving behind family and friends and traveling to an

People are often forced to migrate within their own country because of hunger or conflict. In 2006, these Sudanese women had to leave their homes in Darfur because of war between the government and rebel groups.

often-unknown destination. It is also expensive, so the decision is not taken lightly. Relatively few people leave their countries even if they are in a desperate situation—the poorest people are seldom the ones to move because they cannot afford to travel.

Pull factors are the things that attract people to the new country. People may hope for a better standard of living and improved healthcare and education services, or they may want to live in a country with more freedoms—to escape from persecution and danger. They may desire a better life for their children. One of the basic reasons for migration is that there is a huge wealth gap between More Developed Countries (MDCs) and Less Developed Countries (LDCs). For example, most immigrants to the U.S. and Canada come from poor countries and are seeking an improved standard of living. But there are just as many people moving between LDCs as there are moving to MDCs.

Forms of immigration

Some people move to another land as migrant workers. They go to earn money for a while and then return home. Immigrants move permanently to seek a better life. They may settle legally by applying to move to their chosen country and being accepted. Others are known as "undocumented migrants" or "illegal immigrants" because they have not entered the country according to the immigration laws. They may have arrived legally on a student or tourist visa (allowing the right to stay for a short time) and stayed on after their visa has run out. Or their situation might have become "illegal" following changes in a country's immigration and residence laws.

People may be forced to escape their country as refugees because they fear for their lives because of war, famine, or persecution. Most refugees are from LDCs and live in other LDCs. Large numbers cross borders to a safer country and stay in refugee camps. The tiny minority able to reach MDCs must apply for asylum (the right to refuge). Sometimes the difference between refugees, migrants, and immigrants is unclear. Some undocumented migrants are refugees who did not know how to claim asylum. Others are asylum seekers whose claim to refugee status has been rejected; these asylum seekers sometimes remain illegally rather than return to their home country.

summary

▶ There are many different reasons why people migrate to another country for a time or immigrate as permanent settlers.

▶ More migrants actually move between LDCs than move from LDCs to MDCs.

▶ Some people believe that More Developed Countries (MDCs) are being "swamped" by immigrants— "foreigners" who cause problems in society.

▶ These people believe it would be better to restrict immigration.

▶ Other people argue that immigrants benefit society and the economy.

CHAPTER 2

The history of immigration

Since the earliest times, people have moved from place to place in search of better farmland or work possibilities. They have also migrated to escape natural disasters, such as floods, earthquakes, or famine, and to flee persecution. Throughout history, when new people arrived in a region they either settled peacefully or fought with the people already living there for control of the area. Sometimes rulers built walls to keep out invaders. In the third century B.C.E., the Chinese emperor, Shih Huang-ti, built the Great Wall of China to stop the neighboring tribes from attacking his lands. The Great Wall stretched 4,500 miles (7,300 km) from east to west. However, until the rise of the nation state (see below), there were no laws to govern who was allowed to live in which country.

Nations arise

Starting from about 1500 onward, countries in Europe began to develop strong, central governments. A sense of national identity arose, along with the growth of national languages and religions. This sense of identity was accompanied by the idea that minority groups living in the countries were outsiders, and did not belong. For example, from the eighth century, much of Spain was under Muslim rule.

▼ Jinshanling Great Wall, 90 miles (140 km) northeast of Beijing, part of the Great Wall of China. The Great Wall was built in many stages over the centuries. A large part of the wall still exists today; nowadays it is a major tourist attraction.

▲ Despite Queen Elizabeth I's attempt to expel the African population of England and Scotland, wealthy people, such as this group on a fishing trip in the 1780s, still kept African servants.

Starting from the twelfth century onward, Christian forces from the north of Spain gradually conquered the Muslim lands. In 1492, Spain was finally united under the Roman Catholic monarchs, King Ferdinand and Queen Isabella. To reinforce the unity of their kingdom in accordance with their religion, they forced out Jewish and Muslim populations that had been living in Spain for centuries.

Another example of the expulsion of people seen as outsiders occurred in England. In the late sixteenth century, there were probably hundreds of Africans living in England and Scotland and working as servants and entertainers. In the 1590s, the harvests failed and poverty increased. The Protestant English queen, Elizabeth I, blamed the Africans for using up resources and declared that as non-Christians they were unwelcome. In 1596 and 1601, she issued orders that all Africans be expelled from England.

viewpoints

"…we order all Jews and Jewesses of whatever age they may be, who live, reside, and exist in our said kingdoms and lordships…that by the end of the month of July next of the present year, they depart from all of these our said realms and lordships…"
From the 1492 *Edict of Expulsion* from Spain, in which King Ferdinand and Queen Isabella accused the Jews of trying to convert Christians to Judaism

"…the Jews…are both in their origin and progress not otherwise to be regarded than under the common circumstance of human nature; if all professions were open to them they would betake themselves to Building, Farming, and all sorts of Improvements like other people."
Irish thinker, John Toland, writing in 1714; Toland believed that Jews should have the same rights as other people

▲ A group of freed slaves, photographed in a town in the southern United States shortly after the Civil War of the 1860s. In 1865, at the end of the war, slavery was abolished in the U.S.

Colonialism and mass migration

Between 1500 and 1800, European powers expanded their trading networks across the world. In order to control the economies of the countries they traded with, they conquered them and became their rulers. This system became known as colonialism. European nations such as England, France, Spain, and Portugal, became colonial nations, and the lands they governed were their colonies.

The slave trade

Starting from the sixteenth century, the Spanish, Dutch, English, and French established vast plantations (farming estates) in the Americas to grow sugar, cotton, and tobacco. They needed large numbers of workers for these plantations. Most of the native populations had either died fighting the colonial powers or from disease, so the European powers enslaved people from their colonies in Africa to work for them. Between 1500 and 1870,

maybe 12 million Africans (the exact figure is not known) were shipped to the Americas from West Africa. The slaves were put to work under cruel conditions on the plantations and labored, unpaid, as miners, soldiers, and shipbuilders. This forced migration—the wrenching of people from their homes and families to be transported across the sea and exploited—became known as the Atlantic slave trade. It continued until the nineteenth century.

Another form of forced migration began in the eighteenth century. From 1788 until 1850, the British government sent convicts (people found guilty of crime) to Australia. Around 160,000 mostly English, but also Scottish and Irish men and women, were transported. Most of them had committed relatively minor offenses but had been convicted several times. They were usually sentenced to between seven and 14 years, although some were sentenced to life in exile. These convicts built communities in Australia.

Between 1850 and 1950, there was a huge wave of voluntary international emigration. This was mostly made up of Europeans leaving for the U.S., Canada, New Zealand, and Argentina in search of a better life. Around 50 to 60 million people emigrated from Europe between 1800 and 1925.

Controls and quotas

Starting from the late nineteenth century, richer nations with industrial economies, such as the U.S., Canada, and Britain, began to introduce laws to keep out immigrants they did not want. For example, in the U.S., the Chinese Exclusion Act became law in 1882. In Britain, the 1905 Aliens Act set a limit on the number of Jews to be allowed in from eastern Europe. The U.S. Immigration Act of 1924 allowed a quota of immigrants from each country, depending on the number of that group already in the U.S. This quota was introduced in an effort to try to keep the proportion of various ethnic groups equal, yet people were allowed to come freely from Mexico and Latin America.

Then, in the 1930s, Europe and the U.S. were plunged into a deep economic crisis that became known as the Great Depression. High levels of unemployment resulted in countries introducing strict controls to limit immigration. Following the rise to power of the German Nazi leader, Adolf Hitler, in 1933 and during the Nazi occupation of much of Europe during World War II, Jews were persecuted and killed. Yet because of immigration controls and anti-Semitism (hatred of Jews), few Jews were given refuge in either the U.S. or the European countries that remained free of Nazi rule.

▲ An elderly Russian Jewish immigrant at Ellis Island, New York, in 1900. All immigrants came here to be checked by officials when they arrived.

World population growth by regions, 1850–1950

	1850 population in millions	1950 population in millions	Average annual growth (%)
Receiving (countries of mass immigration)			
Americas	59	325	1.72
North Asia	22	104	1.57
Southeast Asia	42	177	1.45
Sending (countries of mass emigration)			
Europe	265	515	0.67
South Asia	230	445	0.66
China	420	520	0.21
Africa	81	205	0.93
World	1,200	2,500	0.74

Source: *Atlas of World Population History*

Immigration after World War II

During World War II (1939–45), more than 60 million people from Nazi-occupied Europe became refugees. Some of them were unable to return home afterward. Following the war, the international community established a system to help refugees. The United Nations Refugee Convention of 1951 listed their rights to live, work, and study freely in a safe country. Since then, there have been many wars that have led to large movements of people seeking refuge.

After 1945, in addition to the mass movement of refugees there was a huge movement of migrants who moved to seek a better life. In contrast with the situation in the 1930s, in the 1950s and 1960s European countries experienced a huge labor shortage and needed immigrants to help rebuild their shattered economies. Meanwhile, many former European colonies gained their independence. This was often a process that involved conflict, and the citizens of these colonies suffered from war and poverty. Western European governments encouraged immigrants to come from their former colonies and from southern Europe, the poorer region of the continent. Now mostly non-Europeans were on the move. In the 1950s, the UK, France, and Belgium received 40,000 immigrant workers per year. In 1961, Germany invited "guest workers" from Italy, Yugoslavia, and Turkey to come and work for a few years. After the guest-worker scheme ended in 1973, many workers stayed on in Germany.

From the 1960s onward, the U.S., Canada, and Australia relaxed their immigration laws and allowed in more people from LDCs. For example, in 1967 Canada introduced a points system: potential immigrants were awarded points depending on their education, their fluency in English and French, and on the need for their skills at the time. If they achieved the required number of points they could settle there and it did not matter where they were from.

At the same time in Europe, a decline in economic growth led governments to try to limit immigration. The UK passed restrictive laws in 1962, 1968, and 1971. However, existing immigrants to Europe were not forced to return to their countries of origin. There were further arrivals through family reunification programs, which allowed spouses, parents, and children to join their families. In the late twentieth and early twenty-first centuries, conflict, natural disasters, and poverty in LDCs led to large numbers of people seeking a better life in MDCs.

It's a fact

In the UK in 1960–61, the Conservative government's minister for health, Enoch Powell, recruited Caribbean workers for the National Health Service (NHS). However, in the late 1960s, when the tide had turned against immigration and when the Conservatives were no longer in power, Powell inflamed prejudice against black people and called for a halt to immigration.

▲ A Turkish clothing store in Berlin's Kreuzberg district, which is called "Little Istanbul" because a large community of Turks live there. There are 2.4 million people of Turkish origin in Germany.

case study

Yueksal Tuncay

Yueksal Tuncay came to Germany from Turkey in the 1960s to work for the car manufacturer, Daimler Benz. He came as a guest worker, expecting to stay between ten and 15 years, but he did not go back to Turkey. Yueksal managed to save some money and set up a Turkish bakery in Berlin. Although happy running his own business in Germany, he still feels he is regarded as different: "When I meet an official or a policeman, they see my black hair and to them I am still a foreigner."

viewpoints

"I have set and always will set my face like flint against making any difference between one citizen of this country and another on grounds of his origin."
Enoch Powell, 1964

"It almost passes belief that at this moment twenty or thirty additional immigrant children are arriving from overseas in Wolverhampton alone every week—and that means fifteen or twenty additional families of a decade or two hence…. We must be mad…as a nation to be permitting the annual inflow of some 50,000 dependents."
Enoch Powell, 1968

CHAPTER 3

Is immigration out of control?

All MDCs have witnessed a huge increase in immigration since World War II, and some people believe immigration has gotten out of hand. The increased use and low cost of air travel make it easy for people to move between countries. Many people argue immigration was useful in the past, but now it should stop. For instance, since 1970, the foreign-born population of the U.S. has increased rapidly as a result of large-scale immigration, primarily from Latin America and Asia. As a percentage of the total population, the foreign-born population more than doubled from 4.7 percent in 1970 to an estimated 9.7 percent in 1997 in the U.S.

Views on Immigration

	Good thing %	bad thing %	don't know%
From the Middle East and North Africa			
Great Britain	60	30	10
France	53	45	2
Germany	34	57	9
Spain	67	26	7
Netherlands	46	49	5
Poland	47	43	10
From Eastern Europe			
Great Britain	62	28	10
France	52	47	1
Germany	31	60	9
Spain	72	22	6
Netherlands	50	47	3
From former Soviet bloc			
Poland	44	46	10
From Asia			
U.S.	62	26	12
Canada	77	15	8
From Mexico and Latin America			
U.S.	60	29	11
Canada	78	15	7

Source: Pew Global Attitudes Project, 2005

case study

Fleeing persecution and poverty

Southern Spain is close to Morocco, at the tip of northern Africa. It is the destination of many northern and western African migrants desperate to flee conflict, persecution, or poverty and to reach Europe.

Promise is a 26-year-old woman from Benin City in Nigeria. Her family sent her to find a better life in Europe. Promise paid $7,000 to people smugglers to get her to Morocco. Her journey took three months. She then had to wait five months in Morocco for the sea to become calm enough for her to make the journey to Europe. During this time she spent most of her savings. Many women in Promise's situation are forced to work as prostitutes while they wait to travel the last leg of their journey to Europe.

Promise had heard that pregnant women were not deported (sent back to their country of origin) by the Spanish authorities. She was three months pregnant when she paid a further $1,500 to make the crossing to Spain. She traveled with 35 others in a *patera*, a flimsy raftlike dinghy. Promise now lives in a small town in Andalucia, southern Spain, with her child and three other women from Benin City who were also pregnant when they arrived. But the majority of migrants who reach Spain are sent straight back.

▲ In 1999, these African migrants, five Nigerians and two from the Ivory Coast, hoped to reach Ceuta, a Spanish-ruled town in northern Morocco, in this small boat. However, they were arrested by Spanish police and probably sent back.

According to Eurostat, the statistical branch of the European Union (EU), the population of foreign noncitizens (people who have not become citizens of their new country) living in Western European EU nations was 22.9 million in 2004, or about 5.9 percent of the population. That represents an increase of 56 percent since 1990. And this figure does not include undocumented migrants.

There is also a massive movement of undocumented migrants from Mexico to the U.S. Although experts estimate there are between 250,000 and 300,000 arrivals a year, others think the figure could be as high as one million. In addition, since immigrants tend to have larger families than members of the host population do, the overall population increases even further. In 2006, the U.S. fertility rate (the average number of children a woman has) was estimated at 2.09. Evidence published in 2005 by the Center for Immigration Studies shows Mexican women in the U.S. have an average of 3.5 children.

It's a fact

In 2005, a law known as HR 4437 was passed in the USA making all illegal immigration a crime. It did not offer a way for undocumented migrants already in the U.S. to become citizens. Plans for increased border security included the placing of cameras along the border with Mexico. Using the Internet, people would be able to spot and report people trying to cross the border illegally.

Is immigration manageable?

Other people argue that immigration is less of a problem than many fear. They say most people believe the level of immigration is higher than it actually is. There are about 192 million people living outside their country of birth, which is about 3 percent of the world's population. Around half of all immigrants move to LDCs rather than MDCs.

In the U.S., a major destination for immigrants, the total number of immigrants per year (including the estimated number of refugees and undocumented migrants) is lower than it was in the peak years of immigration to the U.S. in the early twentieth century.

▼ This Latin-American worker is raking blueberries in Maine. Farmers in the U.S. rely on migrant workers for labor.

v i e w p o i n t s

"…Mexicans in particular and Latinos in general contribute an enormous amount to this country [the U.S.]. The most honorable thing you can do with your life is to support your family, and that's what most of these people are doing. They leave their countries to come here and make three bucks an hour, and still send money home…"
Latino actress Eva Longoria, speaking in support of protests in the U.S. by Hispanic groups angry at proposed immigration quotas and possible deportations, 2006

"The courageous heroes on the world scene are not those men and women in poor countries who have the energy, the intelligence, and the skills to escape to a rich country but rather those remaining with their people. Rather than focus on improving conditions for themselves and their families by emigrating, they strive to raise the conditions for whole communities."
Roy Beck, executive director of the NumbersUSA, which campaigns to reduce immigration, June 2006

Since then, the U.S. population has more than doubled. And since those peak years the rate of immigration has fallen by around two-thirds. Although the foreign-born population of the U.S. has increased, in 2006 it was estimated that just 10 percent of the total population was born outside the country. This does not indicate that the country is being "swamped" by immigrants. While newspaper headlines highlight the number of immigrants flooding into a country, there are few headlines about the high level of emigration from MDCs.

People who believe immigration is not a major problem point to the fact that large numbers of undocumented migrants go abroad for several years and then return home. They do not immigrate permanently. This is known as "circular migration" and is typical of Mexican workers. Between 1965 and 1986, it is estimated that around 28 million undocumented Mexicans entered the U.S. Around 23 million of them, the great majority, eventually returned to Mexico. Immigration patterns also change over time. As countries develop, emigration slows down. Large numbers used to emigrate from countries such as South Korea and Ireland, but since these countries have developed their economies, they are now destinations for immigrants.

Big families?

Immigrant families tend to have larger families than do members of the host population. But the evidence shows that the fertility rate falls within a generation or so to match that of the host population. During 1991–98, migrant women in France had an average of 2.5 children compared with 1.7 among native-born French women. Women who had arrived in France

before they reached the age of 13 had only a slightly higher fertility rate, because they adopted the local preference for small families.

Net migration to the 15 countries of the EU in 2003, and to the U.S. in 2000

Country	Migration per 1,000 inhabitants
Austria	4.7
Belgium	3.4
Denmark	1.3
Finland	1.1
France	0.9
Germany	1.7
Greece	3.2
Ireland	7.8
Italy	10.4
Luxembourg	4.7
Netherlands	0.4
Portugal	6.4
Spain	17.6
Sweden	3.2
UK	4.4
U.S.	3.5

Source: *Europe in Figures*, 2005

summary

► Some people are concerned about the increase in the foreign-born population in MDCs.

► Others argue that immigration is manageable.

CHAPTER 4

How does immigration affect the host economy?

Some people maintain that immigrants put pressure on scarce resources in the host country, such as housing, education, and health services. These people argue that immigrants go to richer countries to take advantage of welfare systems that do not exist in their own countries. Then, they say, the new country must pay for the education of immigrants' children and care of their elderly relatives, which is unfair on local people.

Studies carried out in the U.S. in the early 1990s found that immigrants made slightly more use of welfare than did local people. This was because immigrants tended to be poorer. Although unemployment levels among immigrants are similar to the national average in the U.S. and Canada, in Europe levels are generally higher than those of the host population. A report from Sweden in 2006 showed there were higher rates of unemployment among people from immigrant families than among native Swedes, and that immigrants were more heavily dependent on social welfare benefits.

Environmental pressures

The anti-immigration lobby argues that there are environmental effects too. In the U.S., the organization NumbersUSA campaigns to reduce the number of

It's a fact

According to a 2006 survey, undocumented migrants (illegal immigrants) in Italy are generally better educated than native Italians. It found that 41 percent of those aged between 25 and 64 had a high-school diploma (showing they had successfully completed secondary school) compared with 33 percent of Italians in the same age group.

Immigration to European countries, 1999–2004

Year	Country	Percentage born in another country	Origin of largest group
1999	France	6%	Portugal
2003	UK	5%	Ireland
2003	Portugal	2%	Cape Verde
2004	Germany	9%	Turkey
2004	Spain	7%	Ecuador
2004	Italy	3%	Albania
2004	Netherlands	4%	Turkey
2004	Sweden	5%	Finland

Source: Eurostat 2006

immigrants. It argues that immigration has caused a rise in population that has contributed to overcrowding in cities. Problems associated with overcrowding include urban sprawl (the unplanned growth of cities), traffic congestion, crammed schools, and crowded outdoor recreation areas. In rural areas, the growing population contributes to loss of natural habitat and the destruction of prime farmland. In addition, greater numbers of people put pressure on limited energy and water supplies.

Some U.S. environmentalists are particularly concerned because people in the U.S. consume resources at the highest rate of any country in the world. Therefore, the increase in the U.S. population has a dramatic effect on the use of the world's resources.

The extremists' response

In several European countries, right-wing extremist groups have taken up people's concerns about population increase and

expressed them in extreme terms. In 2006, the Italian government announced a plan to give legal status to 350,000 undocumented migrants who were working and had lived in the country for at least five years. Robert Calderoli, a senior member of the Northern League, a far-right political group, claimed this would lead to "an invasion" of migrants. Earlier he had said that Muslim immigrants were stealing jobs and homes from native Italians and that all undocumented migrants should be sent back to their country of origin. Some people say unless governments limit immigration, such views will become more popular and there will be growing conflict between local people and immigrants over access to resources, such as housing.

▼ A migrant worker and his family, near Watsonville, California. Migrant workers are often paid low wages and forced to live in cramped conditions.

▲ Some people believe unemployed workers, such as these people standing in line at an unemployment office in Pontiac, Michigan, have been put out of a job by immigrant workers.

Competing for jobs

Although the birthrate is declining in Europe, there is unemployment. Anti-immigration campaigners argue therefore that it is wrong to allow in large numbers of newcomers. Migration Watch UK is a pressure group that wants a reduction in immigration. Its chairman, Sir Andrew Green, noted in 2006 that although Britain had a strong economy, 4.2 million people were unemployed or receiving disability benefits because they could not work. Green said letting in foreign laborers makes it difficult for the government to reach its goal of returning one million Britons to work. Immigrants compete for jobs with local people, who lose their jobs or remain unemployed.

Such campaigners argue that this problem becomes more severe when the economy is doing badly and fewer workers are needed. According to Professor Vernon M. Briggs of Cornell University, the number of undocumented migrants (estimated at 11.5 to 12 million in the U.S. in 2006) is the real problem. They take work from young people looking for their first job and from older ethnic minority workers with few skills.

A related argument is that immigrants are prepared to work for lower-than-average wages. This allows employers to reduce wages in general for all workers. One economist, George Borjas of Harvard University, maintains that poorly educated men who had dropped out of high school saw their earnings decrease by 7.4 percent between 1980 and 2000 as a result of the competition they face from immigrants for employment.

European Union expansion

In May 2004, the European Union expanded to include ten more countries, increasing the total number of its member states from 15 to 25. At first, only the UK, Ireland, and Sweden allowed in immigrants from the new EU nations as part of an agreement to permit freedom of travel within the union. By August 2006, more than 427,000 immigrants had arrived in the UK from the new member states—significantly more than the 13,000 a year predicted by the government.

One of the immigrants, a 30-year-old hairdresser, Agnieszka Skretkowicz, came to London from Poland because she could not make a living at home. "I love Poland; it's a beautiful country," she says, "but it's hard there." In 2006, Finland, Spain, and Portugal announced they would lift restrictions on eastern European immigrants. Migration Watch UK asserts that unless Germany, France, Austria, and Italy also open their doors, the UK could be overwhelmed with immigrants, especially when Romania and Bulgaria join the EU in 2007.

It's a fact

Out of more than 427,000 Eastern European workers in the UK in 2006, 82 percent were aged between 18 and 34. Of these, 1,777 had applied for income support because they could not earn enough money to live on, while 3,519 had applied for unemployment benefits because they had lost their jobs.

▼ This Filipino man works on a Norwegian car ferry. In order to work in Norway for more than three months, people from outside the Nordic countries need to have a special work visa for their type of job.

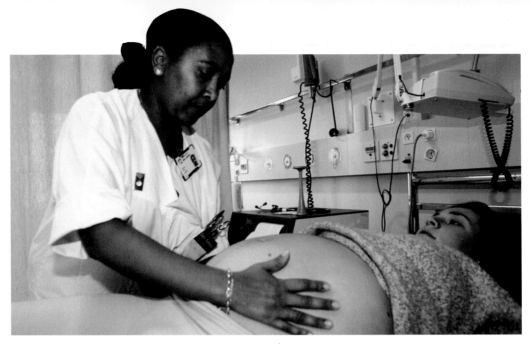

▲ Sara, a Somali migrant, works as a midwife in a hospital in Oslo, Norway. There are many vacancies for nurses in Norwegian hospitals. For locals it is a low-paid job, but for migrants from LDCs the salary seems high.

Contributing to the national wealth

Those people in favor of immigration argue that both skilled and unskilled immigrants give more than they take from the economy in the long term. The U.S. National Academy of Sciences has found that each immigrant, with his or her descendants paying taxes, will contribute $80,000 to the national budget. Undocumented migrants, who avoid contact with the authorities so they are not detected, receive no welfare benefits yet still pay tax. In the U.S., for example, some of them have fake social security numbers in order to get jobs, and so they pay tax on their earnings. They pay sales tax on clothes, gasoline, and other goods they buy. Therefore, immigrants help pay for housing, education, and welfare.

The pro-immigration lobby argues that because governments benefit from the immigrants' contribution, they should use taxes sensibly to ease the stress on scarce resources. They should plan urban development and provide public transportation to ease traffic problems. They should build enough houses and schools, and protect farmland.

case study

A low-paid worker in London

A survey published in 2005 showed that most cleaners on London's Underground (subway network) were from African countries, especially Nigeria and Ghana. Kobena is a university graduate from Ghana. Since arriving in the UK in 2003, he has worked as a cleaner on the Underground for 54 hours a week. He earns the official minimum wage of £5.05 (about $9.50) per hour, much less than half the average earnings in the city. The job allows only 12 days' paid vacation a year and no sick pay. Kobena even has to pay to travel on the Underground to do his job. He supports four children in the UK and also sends money to his family in Ghana. Kobena feels his employer shows no concern for workers' welfare: "They just want us to work."

Employment

Pro-immigration campaigners state that the number of jobs in the economy is not fixed, so it is untrue that immigrants take work away from locals. They say that immigrants often create new businesses and provide jobs. In most countries, foreign workers tend to take low-paid jobs in construction, agriculture, and in the service industries—jobs that locals do not want. They may take these low-paid jobs even if they are highly qualified. They fill in the gaps in the workforce. For example, in the UK and Scandinavia they take up vacancies in the health and education sectors. In 2002–3, more than 40 percent of new nurses registered in the UK came from overseas. Much of the hotel industry in London and around the country relies on the labor of undocumented workers.

Even when unemployment is high, it is argued, immigrants do not make the problem worse. Local people who lose their jobs will probably draw unemployment benefits until they are able to find suitable work. Immigrants in this situation are more likely to take on any casual work they can find, for example, as cleaners or laborers on construction sites.

▼ A polish plumber working in a London house: between May 2004 and June 2006, Polish people made up more than half of migrants to the UK from EU states.

Surveys in MDCs such as Germany, Australia, Canada, the U.S, and the UK have concluded that an influx of immigrants makes little difference to employment or wage levels for the host population. In the U.S., a 2006 study found that immigrant workers complement rather than compete with U.S.-born workers. The foreign-born workers occupy the lowest-paying, unskilled jobs while the U.S.-born workers move onto more rewarding jobs.

Boosting the working population

Europe's population is declining. In the EU the average fertility rate is 1.4 children per woman, but a country needs an average fertility rate of 2.1 children per woman to maintain its population at the same level. The European population is also aging, which means there is an increasing number of old people compared with people of working age. Countries need large numbers of workers to pay taxes toward pensions for the elderly and to care for them. Immigrants, who are mostly young, can help address the labor-shortage problem. So, the pro-lobby argues, it is right to allow in immigrants.

Spain has the lowest fertility rate in Europe (1.2 children per woman). In 2005 it had 3.7 million immigrants, representing 8.5 percent of the population. The largest immigrant group is from Ecuador. Ecuadorians have been coming to Spain since a severe economic crisis hit their country in 1999. They speak Spanish and integrate easily into the workforce. Officially there are 476,000 Ecuadorians in Spain, but there are also many undocumented migrants. The women often work as housekeepers and nannies, while Ecuadorian men work in industry, construction, commerce, and agriculture.

Reducing the labor shortage

The situation in Spain is typical of European countries. The French Institute of International Relations has predicted that Europe must admit 30 million immigrants by 2020 or face a drop in the production of goods, which would damage its economies. The MDCs are trying to recruit skilled migrants to fill labor vacancies. For example, an immigration law introduced in Germany in 2005 aimed to encourage highly skilled foreign workers to settle in the country. The host countries benefit because they have not had to bear the costs of educating and training their new workers.

Outside Europe, other MDCs depend on immigrant labor. Australia has the highest foreign-born population of any MDC—almost one in four of its people. Yet a report by a leading business information company in 2006 stated that the country needed to increase its intake of immigrants further to maintain economic growth.

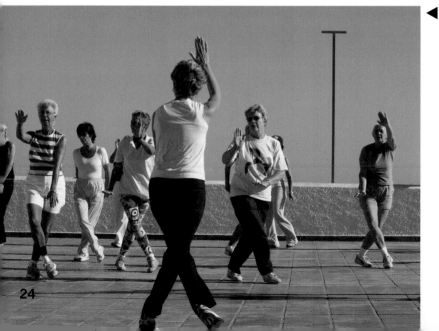

◀ Some people move to Spain from Northern European countries, such as these immigrants near the Costa Blanca. They usually immigrate because of the warm weather and comfortable lifestyle rather than because of work opportunities.

▲ MDCs are trying to encourage highly skilled workers, such as IT experts, to enter their countries.

summary

▶ Some people argue that immigrants take resources away from local people, and add to pressure on the environment. Immigrants are prepared to work for lower wages than local people, which means that the latter, particularly the poorly educated, lose their jobs to immigrants.

▶ Other people argue that immigrants are good for the host economy and that they do not take away jobs from local workers. In fact, they often create businesses and increase job opportunities. They help boost the working population, which is useful in countries where the population is declining.

viewpoints

"The impact of immigration in mitigating [reducing the problem of] population aging is widely acknowledged to be small, because migrants also age."
UK Home Office Research Department

"Immigration…can help sustain overall numbers…and help rejuvenate the population [increase the numbers of young people].… Nevertheless, the rejuvenation effect does not persist. Immigrants, when faced with the social and economic pressures of living in a richer country, soon pick up local habits and opt for smaller families.… So while immigration can help slow population decline and aging, in most cases it will only be able to do this to a limited extent."
Peter Stalker, specialist in international migration

CHAPTER 5

What are the effects of emigration?

It is argued that emigration deprives LDCs of their best educated and highly skilled workers. This is called the "brain drain." Many countries have lost large proportions of their qualified citizens; for example, one-quarter of Ghanaian and Iranian graduates have emigrated from their native countries.

The impact of the brain drain

The migration of more than 20,000 health professionals a year from sub-Saharan African countries is a serious problem. These nations are suffering from increasing poverty and the effects of HIV/AIDS, and require increased numbers of health workers. Yet they are losing many of these to HIV/AIDS and to emigration. While the LDCs have paid to educate and train these workers, the MDCs are benefiting from their skills. The departure of qualified people has an effect on the long-term development of the poorest countries. Some people argue that it is not ethical for MDCs to recruit them.

The "brain drain" in small Caribbean countries is the highest in the world. Here it has a significant effect because the populations are so much smaller than those of large sending countries such as India and China. In 2004, 75 percent of Jamaicans with a degree lived outside the country (60 percent of them had migrated to the U.S.). As a result, there is a huge shortage of nurses and teachers in Jamaica.

Disruption of society

On an individual level, emigration disrupts family life for those remaining at home.

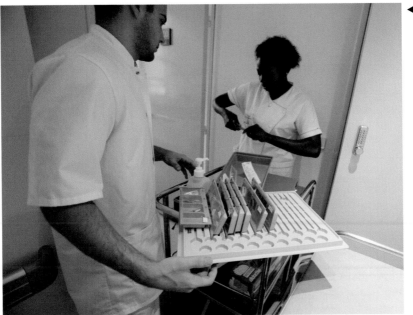

◄ There is a great shortage of nurses in Western countries. Hospitals such as this one in Paris, France, rely on immigrant nurses to staff their wards.

▲ This Chinese family lives in Australia. China is one of the main sources of emigrants worldwide, and there are Chinese people living in almost every country. Most Chinese migrants today are highly skilled professionals.

Women are often left to support their families, but many also migrate, leaving children to be cared for by grandparents, older siblings, or friends. It is extremely hard for families to be separated in this way. Some experts argue that although people should have the right to emigrate, qualified workers should be able to lead a successful life in their own country.

The money sent home by migrants is clearly a major source of income for families. According to a 2003 World Bank report, in some rural areas of Jamaica 40 percent of households receive income from family members working abroad. While this can help individual families and communities, and sometimes may fund small business ventures, it does not necessarily spur economic growth and development at a national level. Also, it tends to encourage people to emigrate in search of a higher income when it could be more beneficial for them to stay and invest in their home country.

viewpoints

"The positive effects of remittances [money sent home] at the household level are clear, although not always undisputed. Unlike government-to-government aid, most remittances go directly to the family budget and are often used for basic subsistence needs [for example, food] and better housing."
Bimal Ghosh, International Organization for Migration, 2006

"…sometimes the best and the brightest leave. That has implications on the delivery of critical services, especially in the health sector; it has implications also for the intellectual capital [educated people] that the country needs for its own development."
Dilip Ratha, a World Bank senior economist and expert on the brain drain, 2006

Remittances

People who emigrate from LDCs generally send a large part of their earnings home to their families—these money flows are called remittances. In 2004, $144 billion—75 percent of remittances worldwide—went to LDCs. And this is just the amount sent through official banking channels. Studies show that perhaps the same amount again is sent through informal channels, for example, with friends. Migrant workers in MDCs earn far more money than they can at home, even in relatively low-paid jobs. For example, professional Filipinos can earn more as cleaners in Europe than in their chosen careers in the Philippines.

Remittances can enrich not just families but whole communities. In African countries, receiving families will at first spend more on basics, such as food and household goods.

As the money continues to flow in, they spend it on health and improving their children's education. They may also invest in land or housing to provide some security for the family's future. People may pool their remittance money and use it to improve their community. In Mexico in the 1990s, farming communities invested in agricultural equipment, which helped them increase production.

It could be argued that the sending of remittances is bad for the host country. It would be better for the economy if the immigrants spent all their money there. However, the immigrants buy goods and services in the country they are living in, which helps boost economy.

▼ In Nattiobannigaripalle in India, a project in the early 2000s provided piped water and installed irrigation channels to water the rice fields. This project was supported by remittances.

case study

A better future?

Pozorrubio is a farming town in the Philippines. The people used to make a living there growing sugarcane, rice, and coconuts. But now they depend on remittances sent home by family members living and working abroad. As the former mayor, Noli Venezuela, comments: "Now we grow big houses. This one's owned by a maid in Hong Kong. Across the street, she's a nanny in Canada." There is a new park, paid for by maids, nannies, and nurses working in Hong Kong. Filipino workers in Los Angeles have bought supplies for the hospital in Pozorrubio. The town has many new stores and businesses, financed by remittances. Paying for education is a high priority too. Ms. Salazar worked as a maid abroad and was able to use her earnings to send all of her five children to college. She says, "Education is the reason we make this sacrifice. It hurt me to leave my children, but I did it to give them a better future."

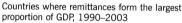

Largest recipients of remittances, 1990–2003

Countries where remittances form the largest proportion of GDP, 1990–2003

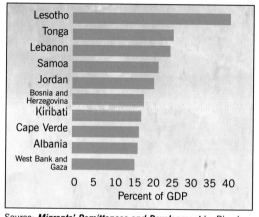

Source: *Migrants' Remittances and Development* by Bimal Ghosh, International Organization for Migration, 2006

Exporting talent

Some countries, such as India, produce more graduates than the economy requires, so emigration makes sense. India is a large country with a population of 1 billion, so the loss of a small proportion of its graduates does not necessarily have a negative effect on its economy. According to British migration expert Peter Stalker, around 25,000 graduates of the seven Indian Institutes of Technology, all prestigious institutions, are working in the U.S.. The export of talent may not represent a permanent loss. Some immigrants eventually return home with their skills and wealth.

summary

▶ The brain drain means LDCs lose highly skilled workers, which hinders their national economic development. It also causes disruption to family life.

▶ Emigration helps LDCs because emigrants send remittances that help improve the living standards of their families and local communities. It also provides opportunities for skilled people abroad who cannot find a job in their own country.

CHAPTER 6

Controlling immigration

Many people are concerned about "opening the floodgates" and allowing in too many immigrants. Hortensia Barderas, a Spanish librarian living in Madrid, holds typical opinions and expresses the dilemma between what is fair and what is practical. She says Spain should not keep people out on the basis of where they are from. However, she says: "if we let everyone in, if we open the doors completely, then we'll be overrun." This viewpoint suggests that governments might want to limit the numbers allowed in and stop undocumented migrants from entering the country.

EU countries may need to work together to control immigration. Some people argue that if one country fails to implement tough measures against undocumented migrants, then large numbers of immigrants will go there. If undocumented migrants succeed in entering Europe and are not deported (sent back), they will be able to travel freely throughout the EU. For example, the Spanish government estimated that 7,000 undocumented African migrants entered Spain between January and June 2006. In July 2006 the EU agreed to help Spain and other southern European countries stem the flow of migrants to their shores.

▼ Border patrol officers arresting undocumented Mexican migrants in Texas along the border between the U.S. and Mexico.

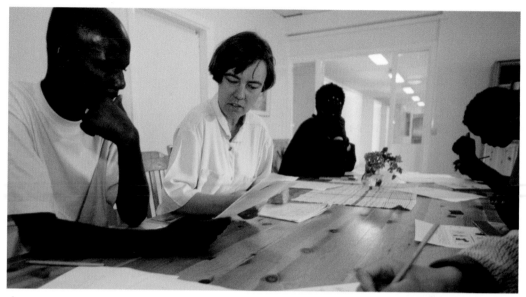

▲ Newly arrived immigrants to Sweden are held in a reception center while officials decide if they can stay in the country. Here, Somali and Iraqi immigrants learn Swedish.

There are similar arguments in the U.S. According to the Pew Hispanic Center's estimate, up to one million undocumented migrants enter the U.S. every year. Some people say the U.S. needs to tighten security along its border with Mexico, where most immigrants enter.

Highly skilled and integrated

People who argue for strict immigration controls believe governments should only recruit those workers who are particularly needed for the country's economy. For example, in Australia and Canada there are skilled-worker programs to allow the controlled entry of highly qualified immigrants. In Germany there is a ban on the recruitment of unskilled and even moderately skilled workers. Highly skilled workers, however, can obtain a permanent settlement permit upon entering Germany.

It's a fact

In order to become an Australian citizen, a person must be a permanent resident of Australia and to have lived in the country for at least two of the past five years. He or she must intend to reside there, be of good character, have a basic knowledge of English, and understand the privileges and responsibilities of citizenship.

Alongside these strict immigration controls, rights to services such as health and education have been restricted in some countries so not all immigrants can gain access to them. As well, governments in the UK, Germany, and the Netherlands have introduced "citizenship tests" to try to ensure immigrants share the values of the host population. An opinion poll in Germany in 2006 showed 79 percent of Germans agreed that such tests were a good idea.

"We will decide who comes to this country, and the circumstances under which they come."
Australian Prime Minister John Howard (who has presided over a carefully controlled migration program based on quotas) speaking in 2001

▲ Hispanic migrant workers in Sonoma County, California, picking and cutting grapes for producing wine.

"Freedom of movement should be the new common sense. It is hard to see why people should not be allowed to move around the world in search of work or safety or both."
Teresa Hayter, human rights activist and author, 2002

Open the borders

There are some who argue there is no need to tighten immigration controls. A few even argue that they are completely unnecessary. They hold there are ethical as well as economic reasons why immigration rules should be relaxed to make it easier for people to move legally from country to country. They argue that MDCs have an important role in the world economy and are in some ways responsible for the continuing poverty in many LDCs. Also,

some say the former colonial powers still have some responsibility toward the citizens of their former colonies.

Pro-immigration campaigners claim that fears of "floods" of immigrants are exaggerated. The decision to migrate is very difficult and there would not be a huge wave of immigrants if controls were loosened or abandoned. Campaigners say there are strong humanitarian reasons for accepting migrants—it is important to protect people fleeing from conflict and persecution. MDCs have all signed international treaties that commit them to defend human rights and offer protection to refugees and asylum seekers. Many people therefore see immigration controls as unfair and even racist. They believe it is unethical not to allow people into a country if they are fleeing persecution or other dangers in their country of origin. Some people are welcomed in Europe, while others are rejected. In the Netherlands, only immigrants from outside the EU, North America, and Australia have to pass the citizenship test. In 2006, Spain announced that workers from the new EU states, such as Poland and Hungary, were permitted to come to Spain, while at the same time it turned away thousands of African migrants.

Unfair on the unskilled

Restrictive laws mean it is extremely difficult for unskilled people to move legally to MDCs, so they are forced to seek an illegal route. Many argue this is unjust. People only try to move to places where there is work, and where there are always jobs for unskilled workers when they arrive. Immigrants come to make a living, and if there are no jobs there will be no mass arrivals. Undocumented migrants often have to pay a people smuggler a vast sum of money to arrange a dangerous and uncertain journey to reach a MDC. And, even if they manage to reach their destination safely, they have to remain hidden from the authorities.

▼ Thousands of Nigerian women like Joy, in Barcelona, Spain were trafficked—tricked into migrating by the offer of a good job—only to be forced into prostitution on their arrival. They are undocumented migrants and hidden from the authorities, so it is hard for them to escape.

Undocumented migrants cannot complain to the authorities about their working conditions because they are not legally resident in a country. This means they are frequently exploited by employers. For instance, a researcher in New York found a Chinese seamstress working more than 100 hours a week for less than $2 an hour. Immigrants often work without breaks, for six or seven days a week, with no healthcare if they get sick. Their human rights are not respected.

Sometimes countries grant amnesty to undocumented migrants, giving them legal status. In 2005, Spain granted amnesty to 570,000 illegal migrants, the sixth amnesty in 20 years. Some people argue it is sensible and ethical to allow all immigrants to live legally in their host country. Then they can have access to education and healthcare, learn the new language properly, and play a more active role in society as well as being happier citizens.

summary

▶ Many people believe strict immigration controls are necessary to limit the numbers of immigrants and to allow in only highly skilled workers. Without such controls, the MDCs could be overrun with immigrants.

▶ Others argue workers will move wherever there are jobs and it is better to allow freedom of movement. There are important humanitarian reasons for allowing people to immigrate to escape persecution and live a better life.

CHAPTER 7

Does immigration cause racism?

There is a view that states that if a country allows in a large number of immigrants it can lead to a rise in racial tension. Local people may feel threatened by the newcomers because they are different. They may resent the immigrants in the belief that they are competing for resources and jobs.

Cultural differences

Much of the debate about immigration and race today focuses on cultural differences between the newcomers and the host population. For example, in many Western nations, some people are wary of accepting more Muslims because they say they do not easily assimilate—fit in with

It's a fact

The number of Muslims in France exceeds six million, representing 10 percent of the population. Muslims in France come from 53 countries and speak 21 languages. Algerians represent a great majority of the Muslims in France.

Some estimates show that the number of Muslims in France will grow more than threefold between 2006 and 2020. Their numbers will reach 20 million owing to the high fertility rate and birthrate, continuous immigration into France and the adoption of Islam by large numbers of French people. As of 2006, Muslims of purely French origin amounted to 100,000.

▼ In 2004, French Muslim women and their supporters demonstrated against the planned law to ban the wearing of the *hijab* (traditional head covering) in French schools. Despite opposition, the law was introduced.

▲ Jean Marie Le Pen, leader of the extreme right-wing National Front party in France, addressing his supporters. His party opposes immigration.

existing society. The newcomers develop their own separate schools, stores, places of worship, and community activities. Muslim women who follow Islamic custom wear a *hijab*, a headscarf, which clearly marks them as different from the majority. France is a secular (nonreligious) country by law. In 2004, the French government reinforced the secular principle by introducing a law that prohibited students from wearing the Muslim *hijab*, the Jewish *yarmulka* (skull cap), and large Christian crosses in schools. This has led to a clash between the authorities and Muslims in particular, and rising racial tension between Muslims and non-Muslims.

Racism and the far right

Some people assert that the expansion of immigrant communities encourages the growth of extreme right-wing political parties. Then, they argue, far-right politicians link immigration to race in order to whip up fear and gain support for their views. Such politicians blame the problems in society on nonwhite immigrants and people of immigrant origin who are actually citizens of the country. For instance, in 1995 in France, Jean-Marie Le Pen, the leader of the far-right Front National (National Front) party, famously claimed that sending back three million immigrants would provide jobs for three million French people. Yet such politicians appear to be less concerned about the large number of other European, white Australian, or American immigrants living in their country. Some people believe the introduction of immigration restrictions could stop the growth of far-right parties that play on people's fear of foreigners. Therefore, they argue, tight immigration controls are morally justified.

Wider issues cause racism

Some people do not agree that immigration causes racism. They believe it has historical causes. Between 1500 and 1900, Europeans enslaved Africans to work for them in the Americas (see page 10). Many Europeans developed the theory that white people were more intelligent than black people, and were born to rule. As European powers conquered countries around the world and ruled them as colonies, this viewpoint spread. Although the colonies gained independence in the twentieth century, for a minority of people the idea of white superiority has lived on.

Racism can also arise from current issues. Since the attacks on the World Trade Center in New York in September 2001, the U.S. has led a "war on terror" in an attempt to root out Islamic extremists in the world. The recent terrorist attacks have fueled a general suspicion of Muslims in western countries. Making a negative judgment about people simply because they are Muslim is a form of racism, known as Islamophobia.

case study

Intolerant outburst

"A racist who branded a Muslim shopkeeper a terrorist on the day of the London bombings has been jailed. James McKeown, 37, of no fixed address, launched a tirade of abuse after spotting Mohammed Mahmood, who was wearing traditional Muslim dress, as he walked along Victoria Road, Cambridge, on July 7. McKeown shouted: 'Look what you've done to London you terrorist, go back to your own country,' before following him along the road hurling further abuse and threatening him with violence. Police said the incident was an unprovoked attack on a 'very calm, quiet man,' and welcomed McKeown's prison sentence. The 37-year-old was convicted of racially aggravated harassment at Cambridge Crown Court and jailed for 130 days."

(*Cambridge Evening News*, December 16, 2005)

▼ French police arresting suspected rioters in Paris in 2005. It was mostly young black and Arab people of immigrant background who rioted in fury about their job prospects.

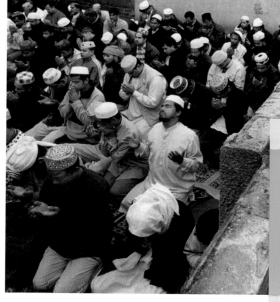

▲ British Muslims at prayer in the backyard of a mosque in Oldham, northern England.

Sometimes, governments blame immigrants for social problems to draw attention away from their own failures. When this happens, people may turn against immigrants, and there is a rise in racism. In 2005, riots broke out in France among black and Arab immigrant communities. The rioters were angry about the lack of jobs and opportunities they faced owing to racial discrimination. Government minister Nicolas Sarkozy (himself the son of a Hungarian immigrant) claimed the riots were caused by mass immigration. He introduced proposals to make it much harder for unskilled immigrants to settle in France and said people who did not like the country could leave. In this atmosphere, public opinion polls showed growing support for the Front National.

summary

▶ Some people say a high level of immigration leads to increased racism.

▶ Other people maintain there are wider historical and political causes of racism.

CHAPTER 8

Does immigration benefit society?

There are people who argue that a large number of immigrants can have a negative effect on society. Newcomers may have different customs and religions that conflict with local habits and alter the character of an area. Immigrants may find it hard to integrate at school and work, especially if they do not speak the language of the host country. For example, Chinese immigrants in the U.S. and Australia, especially older people, struggle to learn English. According to a 2006 survey by Radio Netherlands, "some 58 percent of Europeans regard ethnic minorities as a threat." Italy, Belgium, and the Czech Republic score above the European average in their dislike of ethnic minorities.

High levels of immigration can divide the population. For example, U.S. cities are segregated—different groups of people live in separate areas. Hispanics are spread throughout the U.S., but they live overwhelmingly in neighborhoods where they are the largest minority group. This kind of segregation is bad for society and can lead to tensions between different communities.

▼ Around the world there are Chinatowns in many major cities, areas in which Chinese restaurants and stores can be found. This photo is of Chinatown in Philadelphia.

▲ This is a Hispanic neighborhood in Los Angeles, California, where the majority of inhabitants are from Latin American countries.

Crime and social problems

Some people say immigrants, especially undocumented migrants, are responsible for crime and threaten social order. Anti-immigration campaigners in the U.S. claim immigration has resulted in a wave of violent crime. For example, in June 2003 it was reported that Adrian George Camacho shot dead a police officer who had stopped his car. Camacho was a Mexican who had been in prison for attempted murder and drug offenses. Some people commented that if the borders had been more tightly controlled, criminals like Camacho would not have been able to get into the country.

Such campaigners argue that social problems result from immigration. In Sweden, for example, unemployment levels are higher among the foreign-born than among natives of the country. Young immigrant people are more likely to drop out of school. Adult immigrants tend to be

It's a fact

Population data from 41 U.S. states indicates that the average non-Hispanic white person lives in a neighborhood that is 6.3 percent Hispanic. But the average Hispanic person lives in a neighborhood that is 44 percent Hispanic.

This kind of segregation can last for generations. Sociologist John Logan, who analyzed the data, noted that the segregation of Jews and Italians in the U.S. declined after about 50 or 80 years. It could take until 2050 before Hispanics begin to be more integrated into U.S. society.

more dependent on social welfare (such as unemployment benefits), and are less likely than native people to vote in local elections. Their communities also experience a higher crime rate.

Those who oppose immigration insist that, while people may want to emigrate to escape suffering in their own countries, governments must put the rights of their existing citizens first.

▲ Hasidic Jews stick closely to ancient Jewish religious traditions and live in their own communities. Most people in Europe and the U.S. are accepting of Hasidic Jews and their rights to follow their own traditions.

In contrast to the view that immigrants are responsible for crime, some people reason that immigrants are just the same as other groups in society. Such people argue that while a few immigrants may commit crime, the vast majority are law-abiding people. More immigrants are arrested, but this is a result of discrimination by the police not the fact that they commit more crimes. And, while a tiny minority of immigrants may sympathize with terrorism, people argue that the perceived recent growth of terrorism is an extreme response to the wars led by the U.S. and the UK against Muslim countries such as Afghanistan and Iraq.

People also argue that there are good reasons why immigrants tend to use more welfare services. In Sweden, immigrants experience higher rates of unemployment because most of them are refugees. In 1972, the Swedish government halted the immigration of workers from non-Nordic countries. Many of the refugees now come from the former Yugoslavia and, to a lesser extent, Iran and Iraq. It takes longer for these people to be integrated into society. They are generally poorer, which is why they rely more on social welfare. In time, it is argued, they will be able to make their contribution to society.

▲ World-famous conductor Zubin Mehta conducting the Vienna Philharmonic Orchestra. Mehta moved from Mumbai, India, to the U.S. when he was 18.

Segregation or integration?

Time is important in the case of segregation too. In the past, similar complaints about immigrants and alien cultures were expressed against the Jews and Italians in the U.S. For example, between 1881 and 1914, about two million Jews migrated from Russia and eastern Europe to the U.S. Many Americans complained about high numbers of Jews in the poorest areas of New York and about their different style of dress, customs, and religious worship. Yet over time Jewish people became integrated into society and made significant contributions in the fields of law, medicine, science, education, literature, music, movies, theater, and art. Pro-immigration campaigners argue that the same will happen with newer groups of immigrants. They say a humane society should support the right of people to make a better life elsewhere. Many people from MDCs migrate to other countries. It is therefore important that others, if they want to, should be allowed to migrate to MDCs.

It's a fact

Famous immigrants to the U.S. include Elie Wiesel (Romania), scholar of Jewish studies and Nobel Prize winner; the great basketball player Hakeem Olajuwon (Nigeria); the orchestral conductor Zubin Mehta (India); the former U.S. Secretary of State Madeleine Albright (Czech Republic); the author Isabel Allende (Chile); the movie director Wayne Wang (China); and Jeong H. Kim (South Korea), who created a highly successful technology company.

Loss of national identity

There is a common view that it is important to have a shared culture and loyalty within a country. British journalist Peter Hitchens maintains that immigration to the UK was extremely limited in the past. Now, he says, there is a huge level of uncontrolled illegal immigration "conservatively estimated at 100,000 a year" (2003). He argues that rather than becoming multicultural, Britain now has no culture and all of its traditions are being forgotten. People are concerned that their national identity is on the verge of being lost and "swamped" by foreign influences.

Similar fears are expressed by a large number of Dutch people, particularly with regard to Islam. According to a 2004 survey by Radio Netherlands, out of 1,020 native Dutch people, 50 percent said they were afraid of Islam and its influence on Dutch society. In the Dutch town of Alphen Aan Den Rijn, employment-office worker Ibolya Fransen believes Muslims, with their own stores and places of worship, are threatening her way of life: "In my town, we have a population of 70,000, but we already have two mosques. In five years' time it will be three or four. They will take over."

▲ In 2006, the Essalam Mosque was under construction in the south of Rotterdam in the Netherlands. Once completed, it will be the biggest mosque in Western Europe, holding 1,500 worshippers.

▲ This Roma family, photographed at a Roma campsite north of Paris in 2005, hoped to be able to move to the UK.

"...those residents who have remained in suburbs subjected to the multicultural experiment feel neglected. They believe they have had to cope with carjackings, gang rapes, drive-by shootings, the occasional explosion at the football (soccer), amplified calls to prayer, and gangs of violent young men who boast that they are proud not to be Australian."
From a report on Muslims blamed for crime in Australia, December 2005

In western countries, there have been heightened concerns about terrorism in recent years, following the attacks on the U.S. of September 11, 2001. Some people believe immigrants, or indeed people of immigrant origin, may not be loyal to their host country. The fear is that some of these people may be Islamic extremists who support terrorism. In July 2005, a series of suicide bombings were carried out in London by Muslim men born and brought up in England. In June 2006, seven Muslim U.S. citizens were arrested accused of planning to blow up the Sears Tower in Chicago, Illinois.

"Several thousands of Romani [Roma] migrants on French territory are subjected to policies the basic aim of which is to make them leave France. They live in indecent slum conditions and find themselves repeatedly evicted from their precarious camps and squats, chased to the next municipality—from which they are in turn evicted. In addition, they are subjected to various forms of violence, abuse, harassment, and neglect that result in extreme violations of their rights in almost all fields of life."
From a report on the Roma in France, 2005 (European Roma Rights Center)

A richer society

Countries do not share a single culture but contain a mixture of cultures because of waves of immigration that have taken place over the centuries. Over time, a cultural exchange takes place between local people and immigrants, with each influencing the other. For example, hip-hop music developed in the U.S. from the Jamaican practice of "toasting" (talking or chanting over the rhythms of popular songs). Since the 1980s, hip-hop has spread all over the world, including to Latin America, Asia, and Africa. In Europe, both local people and immigrants produce hip-hop music.

Food is another obvious example. In the multicultural cities of MDCs people can eat food from all around the world. In Chicago it is possible to choose from American hamburger restaurants, Jewish bagel bakeries, Cajun fried-chicken cafés, Spanish tapas bars, Japanese sushi bars (see below), Mexican taco bars, and dozens more styles of food outlets.

▼ Many of the most popular restaurants in western countries, such as this sushi restaurant in the U.S., are run by immigrants.

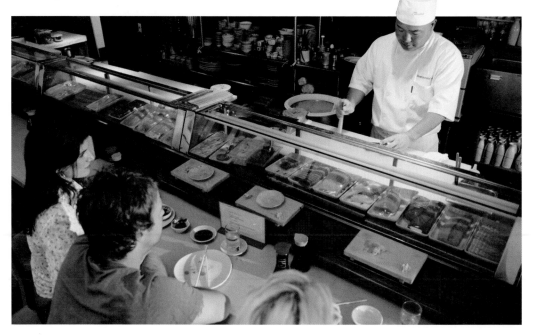

Education

Many believe it is advantageous for children to grow up among people from different cultures. Priya, a sixteen-year-old British Asian, says: "I think mixing people from different backgrounds is a wonderful and crucial thing to do. Wherever somebody lives there will always be different types of people, so mixing them, especially in schools, is vital. By learning about different cultures you have a better understanding of yourself."

Those in favor of immigration say this shows immigrants make a country richer economically and culturally. They say it is important to look at the benefits and remember there has always been international migration, but immigration controls are a twentieth-century development.

▲ Immigrants have brought their music and dance to their new countries. Here, an English couple take a Latin American salsa dance class.

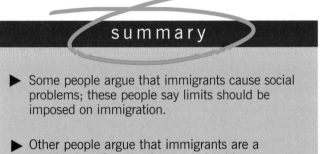

summary

▶ Some people argue that immigrants cause social problems; these people say limits should be imposed on immigration.

▶ Other people argue that immigrants are a positive benefit to society and should therefore be welcomed.

case study

Faïza Guène

Young French author Faïza Guène was born to Algerian immigrants in France. She grew up on the social housing projects in Pantin, outside Paris. At the age of 13, Faïza started to attend the neighborhood cultural center and began to write a novel about a teenage girl growing up with her Moroccan mother in a poor suburb of Paris. Called *Just Like Tomorrow*, the book expressed the hardships of immigrant life but also the positive aspects of life in the suburbs. One of the founders of the center read the first 40 pages of the novel and showed it to his sister, who worked for a publishing company. She was so impressed she put it forward for publication. The book proved extraordinarily successful; 200,000 copies were sold in France and it became required reading in schools in 2006.

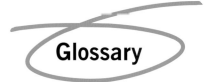

Glossary

Alien Foreign, or from a foreign country.

Amnesty An official pardon for an offense.

Asylum seeker A person who has fled his or her country and is claiming asylum—protection as a refugee in a safe country.

Citizenship Membership of a state, either as a person born there or as an immigrant who has gained membership; citizenship involves certain rights and responsibilities.

Discrimination Treating people unfairly, for example, because of their skin color, religion, gender, or age.

Emigrate To leave one's own country to settle permanently in another.

Ethnic group A group set apart from others because of its national or racial origin or culture.

Front National A right-wing political party in France that opposes immigration.

Ethnic minority A group set apart from the majority in society because of its national or racial origin or culture.

Hispanic A Spanish-speaking person from Latin America or from a Latin American family, living in the U.S.

HIV/AIDS A disease of the human immune system resulting from infection by a virus.

Host population The local people in a country to which immigrants come.

Legal immigrant An immigrant who has permission to settle in another country or an undocumented migrant who has won the legal right to settle.

Less Developed Countries (LDCs) The poorer countries of the world, including the countries of Africa, Asia (except for Japan), Latin America, and the Caribbean.

Migrant worker A person who moves to another country for a limited period to work.

More Developed Countries (MDCs) The richer countries of the world, including Europe and northern America.

Multicultural Involving several ethnic groups and cultures.

Net migration The difference between immigration into and emigration from an area; for example, if 300,000 people enter a country and 200,000 leave, there is net migration of 100,000 into the country.

Nordic Refers to the northwestern European countries of Scandinavia, Iceland, and Finland.

Persecution The cruel treatment of people, for example, because of their race, religion, or political beliefs.

Quota The number of immigrants allowed to enter a country each year.

Refugee A person who seeks safety from war, natural disaster, or ill treatment in another country.

Right wing The side of a political system that is more traditional, including people who generally do not welcome change.

Roma A traveling people who originally came from India but now live mostly in Europe.

Segregation Describes a situation in which different ethnic groups live in separate areas.

Service industries Industries, such as hotels, catering, and transportation, that provide services rather than making goods.

Sociologist A person who studies human society.

Undocumented migrant A person who has not entered the country according to the immigration laws.

United Nations (UN) An organization founded at the end of World War II, with the aim of preventing future wars.

World Bank An international banking organization that makes loans to countries when they have economic problems.

Timeline

3rd century B.C.E. Emperor of China builds a wall to keep out neighboring tribes.

C.E. 1442 Portuguese start to enslave Africans.

1492 Spanish monarchs expel Jews and Muslims from Spain.

c.1550 Europeans start to transport enslaved Africans to the Americas to work.

1596 Queen Elizabeth I orders that all Africans be expelled from England.

1788 British government begins to send convicts to Australia.

From c. 1830 Indentured workers (who have borrowed money), mostly from China, India, and the Pacific region, emigrate to European colonies.

From c. 1850 Voluntary mass emigration to the Americas begins.

1882 Chinese Exclusion Act passed in the U.S.

1901 Immigration Restriction Act in Australia ends non-European immigration; it becomes known as the White Australia Policy.

1905 Aliens Act passed in Britain.

1924 Immigration Act in the U.S. permits the immigration of a quota of people from each sending country.

Post-1945 Mass emigration of Europeans to Australia.

1950s and 1960s France and UK invite immigrants from their former colonies.

1961 Germany invites "guest workers" into the country.

1962 Immigration Act in UK introduces restrictions on immigrants.

1965 Immigration and Nationality Act in the U.S. abolishes the system of national quotas.

1967 Canada introduces a points system for potential immigrants.

1972 Sweden introduces a law to prevent immigrants from non-Nordic countries from entering.

1973 Economic crisis in Europe leads to restrictions on immigration.

1973 End of the White Australia Policy; all immigrants are permitted to apply for citizenship after living in Australia for three years.

1986 U.S. law imposes penalties on employers who hire undocumented migrants and offers an amnesty to three million undocumented migrants already in the country.

1999 Large numbers of Ecuadorians move to Spain because of economic crisis in Ecuador.

February 2004 French government bans schoolchildren from wearing obvious religious symbols, such as the Muslim headscarf.

May 2004 The European Union is expanded from 15 to 25 members; the UK, Ireland, and Sweden permit immigration from the new member countries.

January 2005 Germany introduces a new immigration law that restricts unskilled or semiskilled workers but encourages highly skilled immigrants.

November 2005 British citizenship test for immigrants comes into force.

December 2005 Immigration law HR 4437 is passed in the U.S..

2006 Finland, Spain, and Portugal lift restrictions on Eastern European immigrants from the European Union.

February 2006 The German state of Baden-Württemberg introduces a citizenship test.

March 2006 Language and cultural awareness tests are introduced in the Netherlands.

May 2006 Protests in the U.S. against immigration law HR 4437.

Further Information

Books to read:

Defining America Through Immigration Policy (Mapping Racisms),
Bill Ong Hing (Temple University Press, 2004)

Dividing Lines: The Politics of Immigration Control in America,
Daniel J Tichenor (Princeton University Press, 2002)

Immigration: A Look at the Way the World is Today (Issues of the World),
Ruth Wilson (Stargazer Books, 2005)

Unguarded Gates: A History of America's Immigration,
Otis L Graham (Rowman & Littlefield Publishers, 2006)

Due to the changing nature of Internet links, The Rosen Publishing Group, Inc., has developed an online list of Web sites related to the subject of this book. This site is updated regularly. Please use this link to access the list:
www.rosenlinks.com/ed/immig/

Index